In Earnest

Kuhan Perumynar

BookLeaf
Publishing

Presentation by *BookLeaf Publishing*

Web: www.bookleafpub.com

E-mail: info@bookleafpub.com

ISBN: 9789357614153

First edition 2022

12/09/22

On the precipice

On the eve of new days
I am wont to halt in my tracks,
To seek other paths,
To live other lives.

On the eve of new days
I must fall,
And in so doing, reacquaint myself
With this unwavering edge

Where I must move,
And then trust.
For indecision kills
On the precipice.

13/09/22
Departing

The head and the heart.
Two star-crossed lovers
Searching,
Forever crossing paths and yet
Unable to find one another.

For all those who have come and gone
There is no greater tragedy
Than watching these two

Departing.

14/09/22

Fire is ahead

A spark of flint
Has seeded many a forest fire,
Their transience belied by their wake.

The embers are alive,
The coals may never out,
And complacency fuels many a flame.

Be vigilant,
Take care,
And heed their warning.

Fire is ahead.

15/09/22

A break in the clouds

A break in the clouds
Seems long overdue.
There is no cause for the rain.

Each heavenward gaze
Confirms clear skies
And yet, my clothes are stained.

I feel the droplets
As cloth clings to skin,
There can be no mistake.

It's raining
It's raining
Explaining won't change,
It's raining, right here, today.

I'm raining
I'm raining
Despite what I say,
And thinking won't dry the rain.

16/09/22

Woe is me

Woe is me
Oh tell me why

I am pain
Personified.

A great big heap
Of tragedy

Always seems
To befall me.

Where's my cake?
Where's my prize?

And all the things
That I desire

That I deserve
That I should have

That I have earned
That I have planned

Can't you see
My world's on fire?!

Or could it be
That I'm just tired?

19/09/22

Resistance

After years of being restrained,
Held down,
I sense resistance.
From where, I am not sure.

There was no rallying cry,
No inspirational figure
Urging us onward.

There was no answer co-opted from the heavens,
No panacea discovered
Strewn amongst the weeds.

There was only a call,
So quiet I almost missed it.
An earnest question, asking
What would happen if I tried?

20/09/22

On looking outwards

For all that there is to be found
In those inward depths,
I fear the friendly fire
Of ricochets in an empty chamber.

Impressive in their construction
These walls stand a question mark.
I spend my time safely
Ensconced within their hard embrace.

Scaling these walls
I ponder
Looking outwards.

21/09/22

My favourite days

It is no accident
My favourite days
Are those on which I have
Nothing to say.

22/09/22

A dreary day

A dreary day spent driving
Is not a dreary day.

22/09/22

The limits of vision

The punishment of missed opportunity
Bears the seeds of newer ambitions.

To be so small,
To see so little,
And lambaste ourselves for
Words unspoken,
Actions unmanifested...

We are children, you and I,
Our vision is by definition
Too small, too narrow,
Too tethered
To see.

23/09/22

Friction

Like tectonic plates,
It is from friction
That thought is conceived.
Movement alone does not suffice.

Like tectonic plates,
It is from friction
That this world is conceived.
Erupting. Shifting. Burying.

For all the might of the mountains
We know nothing of the sea.

24/09/22

You cannot get there from here

To know is to think.
To understand is to think less.
To feel is entirely different.
And you cannot get there from here.

25/09/22

I thought of you today

I would have loved for you to have met her,
To see fire embodied
In loving warmth
And the perseverance of will
Echoing throughout a lifetime.
To see what resilience made flesh looks like.

I would have loved for you to have known her.
Asked for her stories,
Really asked,
And listened.
Paid attention to each
Strike of the hammer that
Sculpted diamond from stone.

I would have loved for you to have learned from her.
Not from what she said,
But who she was.
How one can weather storms and remain steadfast.
That one can know pain and suffer,
Truly suffer,
And not harden or break.
That ultimately faith is something you give yourself.

I would have loved that she had met you
As you would stand before her now.
That she could see that things are turning out well,
That her hopes were well-founded,
That her boys are growing up.

And though she is there, and you are here, writing this,
I suspect she already knew.
And someday I hope I do too.
But for now, just know that I thought of you.

28/09/22

From over there

Walking through this world on my shoulders
I forget sometimes, that in many ways,
I am to you what you are to me.

To you, standing over there, looking at me,
I'm curious,
What do you see?

01/10/22

Onward

There will come a time
When things have gone so well for so long
That you will forget that you must fall again.
Do not worry.
It will hurt.
It is inevitable.

You will make a mistake.
Then you will make another.
And nothing you do will stop the next.

In these moments you will be drawn to think,
And evaluate the situation writ large.
You will be drawn to pour over the ruins,
One piece of rubble at a time
To uncover where things went wrong.

Instead, I urge you to look back for a moment,
Not on the fall,
But on all those that came before.

Every decision will bring problems anew.
So choose
And move onward.

02/10/22
Hold on

On days that feel like storms,
When there is a to-do list as long as
The oceans are wide,
And the mind is unwilling,

Force is not your only recourse.
And though you will fortress your mind,
No amount of willpower will be enough
To swim against the rip.

So float,
And hold on.
For the tide is in
And soon it will be out once more.

02/10/22

On friendship

The idea that one can be an island
Is so tantalising to the ego.
Time and time again
I find myself beckoned by its romance.
That all I need exists within this mind and flesh.
That this one person is enough.

I swaddle myself within theory after theory
Exculpating seclusion and self-sufficiency
Until I am safely ensconced within my own walls,
Each assault to the psyche
Just further evidence of the dangers that
Should be fortressed without.

The catharsis of friendship
Comes not from sharing our problems,
But from realising that our problems are shared.
The joy that flows from one friend to another
Is continuous.

The catharsis of friendship
Comes not from forgetting oneself,
But from finding a part of oneself seated in front of us.
Friendship entails the understanding that this life exists as much
Outside of this body as it does within it.

It is the reminder that this world is not singular.
The world on our shoulders is but one of many.
There are others who share these same burdens,
Who will walk this same path
And different ones too.

Friendship is the repeated, undeniable expression of love
That leads to the slow realisation
That our lives are as big as we let them be.
And I am thankful to my friends for the reminder.

06/10/22

On the last mile

I have faltered sometimes
At the finish line.
Having seen the glory that awaits me
I feel in some way, it is already mine.

When the end is in sight
It is so easy to ask of ourselves - Why go there?
I know that I can.
There is nothing left to prove.

I have faltered sometimes
At the finish line.
So entranced by the phoenix that rises
I have overlooked the phoenix that soars.
So spellbound in realising what I am capable of
I have forgotten that I am not that man,
Not yet.

There is much to be said for persevering to the end.
Right to the end.
There is more there.
And the view of the shoreline
Compares not to the feeling of sand beneath your feet.

So, when you see the end,
Go further, push harder.
Do not see the end.
Go there.